NO ONE SWIMS
ALONE

JUDY BROWN

Order this book online at www.trafford.com
or email orders@trafford.com

Most Trafford titles are also available at major online book retailers.

Print information available on the last page.

ISBN: 978-1-4907-8807-4 (sc)
ISBN: 978-1-4907-8808-1 (hc)
ISBN: 978-1-4907-8813-5 (e)

Library of Congress Control Number: 2018938992

Trafford rev. 03/27/2018

 www.trafford.com

North America & international
toll-free: 1 888 232 4444 (USA & Canada)
fax: 812 355 4082

CONTENTS

My appreciation to

Ira Progoff whose Intensive Journal Process I first discovered decades ago, and which has allowed me to trust that I could learn from my own life—and in that learning, I have maintained a daily journal practice from which the poems have emerged.

To the people, and places, who have inspired these poems.

To those who have encouraged the poetry—friends, family, my poetry group, my husband David, and my mentor John Gardner who in the face of my insistence that I was a writer of public policy, said I was also a poet.

To those who have helped create this collection—

My editor Megan Scribner, for her creativity in winnowing and organizing the poems.

My husband David Ward whose production skills make all this possible,

My Mother, Elizabeth Burgess Ball, whose rule about living on the lake, gave birth to the title: No one Swims Alone.

Gratitude to all—

Judy Brown, March 2018

Other books by Judy Brown

The Choice

The Sea Accepts all Rivers

The Leaders Guide to Reflective Practice

The Art and Spirit of Leadership

Simple Gifts

Stepping Stones

Flourishing Enterprise (with others)

Jottings

Journal

Notes

For more details see Judy's web site

www.judysorumbrown.com

Dear Reader,

Franz Kafka had these words for a young friend ambivalent about pursuing a creative life, "Art, like prayer, is a hand outstretched in the darkness, seeking for some touch of grace which will transform it into a hand that bestows gifts."

I hope these poems might be a gift for you. I can only hope.

One of the mysteries, for me as a poet, is how poems that emerge in my morning journal, reflecting some unexpected inner explorations, may turn out to be a gift to stranger or friend. It is a process as mysterious as writing down the poems themselves. What may catch your attention? Why? What words evoke a "yes" for reasons I could never know, never imagine.

So I send these poems off to you, like a note in a bottle, bobbing on the waves, landing eventually on a distant shore—moved by tides and winds—like so much of our lives.

May this collection meet you where you are in your life

Judy Brown, March 2018

OPENING POEM

I will go to the end of the world

This poem
Goes to the
Farthest point—
To the distant horizon—
This poem
Wraps its heart
Around the stranger,
The enemy,
The emissary,
All.
This poem

Knows no resting

Till it arrives

At the end of the world,

With arms full,

Of welcome.

This poem is me

Breathing.

    March 2013,

WINTER

They say God is in the limits

AGAINST THE WIND

How to float

Against the wind

As that lone pelican

Just now did—

Sailing low,

Heading north

Into the roaring

Trade winds,

In the island sun,

Wings stretching out

Precisely,

As if resting,

Gliding.

How can we learn

To harness the

Opposing energy

And ride into it,

Still and calm?

December 24, 2015

ANOTHER STORM

The winter storm that they predicted
Lasted three long days this week.
But just before it hit, I led
A dialogue with doctors
On how to provide wisdom
And good leadership
To people nearing death—
Another storm to be
Anticipated
If we have good sense—
And one like this long
Winter blizzard,

That prepared for,

Can be rich with

Moments of connection,

Love and beauty.

But if the signs of its

Approach are overlooked,

It, like a winter blizzard

Creates crisis, misery, and

Suffering unneeded.

I love preparing for

A storm, the power,

Beauty of it. Whether

It materializes or just

Goes by. There is

A comfort in the readying—

Having good counsel,

Being at home,

Tucked in before

A wood fire in the stove.

That's where

I aim to be.

January 24, 2016,

THIS OTHER WORLD

This other world
Where my pale skin
Makes me invisible,
Unseen, at times—
This other world
Where temperatures
Move from the seventies
At night
To eight-two in daylight,
All year round,
And there are no
Freezing homeless—

This other world

Where houses painted

In what seems

At first to me, such

Garish pinks and

Neon greens

Now seem quite

Natural and beautiful.

This other world

Where mountains

Of pink flowering

Vines and sea grape

Clamor over everything—

The fences

And old rotting

Dump trucks,

Abandoned shacks

And over-done

Huge mansions—

This other world

Where I don't know

The names of birds and flowers,

Nor what one does

With little bags of

Colored peppers—

So I experiment

And learn

To live here

In this other world.

    January 9, 2015,

COUNTRIES IN OUR MINDS

There are countries

In our minds,

Whose boundaries

Keep thoughts

From crossing over,

Wondering.

No passports

To be had;

No possibility

Of exploration,

A geography

Of our own making.

When the child wrote to

God and asked

"Who put

The lines

Around the

Countries?"

She was speaking

To my heart

About my mind.

     December 3, 2005

THE GEOGRAPHIC CURE

If we're not

Settled in

The place within

That is our home,

Changing locale,

Shifting geography

Will only prolong

Misery.

The habits

Keeping us

In chains

Where we now are,

Will travel

With us.

There's wisdom

In not moving

Until we know

The map

Of the terrain

Within.

January 21, 2015

LONGING FOR A POEM

Longing for a poem—

The peeling

Of the layers

Of my day,

My life,

The opening

To inner space

And mystery,

Longing

For that compass,

Longing for that voice.

December 13, 2015

BEING HERE

Being here
Means
I cannot
Be there.
How to grow
At home
With that
Awareness.
They say that
God is in
The limits.

January 14, 2015

RAIN AND SUNSHINE

Rain and sunshine

At one moment—

So life,

Although

We do not

Think it so.

We separate

The two—

The sun, the rain,

The good, the bad

As we call them—

Yet are both

The same—

Just weather—

Life.

From a much

Different perspective,

The makings

Of a rainbow.

     January 4, 2016

THE POETRY APPEARS

The poetry appears
When there is time—
And provocation,
Or reflection,
Or nothing here
But time and space
To notice—
To take note.

                January 10, 2015

OTHERS

Others remind us

Who we are

When we forget—

They open up

The hardened heart

That once made art

But now,

Head down,

Into the winds of life,

Eyes narrowed,

Without pen,

The candle

Still unlit,

Creative footing

Lost, we realize

Others

Remind us

Who we are.

When we

No longer

Find an open page,

Others remind us.

       January 10, 2017

UNSAID

You've lost him now—
Too sad for words—
But what if he knew now—
As if he listened to your heart,
Your every word unsaid:
How much you treasure him,
And think of him—
His wisdom and the
Difference that he made—
The way he touched your life.
Would tears fall freely then—
Not of regret but simply

Of the joy of knowing him?

That being said,
Don't make
That same mistake
Again.

      January 8, 2017

WHY HESITATE?

Why hesitate—
What if the offer
I am holding back
Is but a gift—
What if my intuition
Yet unspoken
Is a golden path
Pointing the way
Through darkest wood
To someplace
Not yet knowable

Nor named?

What if the

Thought I hold

In silence—

So unsure it is

Of value—

Is a key

For all of us

To carry

For a lifetime—

A key to doors,

To gates,

That we have yet

To stand before?

Why hesitate

To offer it?

Why then hold back?

December 9, 2016

SELF INDULGENT

Thinking

Seems too

Self-indulgent—

Like resting—

Or writing poetry—

Taking long walks.

The world's in agony.

Can one show care

By being quiet

Or by reaching out

In gentle ways—

Or only through

Outrage,

Anxiety

And fear?

What shape takes

Solidarity

These days?

Can love

Be quiet?

December 31, 2015

LOVE AND FEAR

Geese glide by
In the dawning sun—
My brother's full
Of good spirits,
And lots of work—
My daughter is
Out hiking
With her love—
Our house is warm
With health, appreciation.
How odd that
I should feel fear

Because a lunatic

Is holding

Anti-Muslim rallies

In the south—

And yet I am afraid.

I know

What threatens any of us,

Threatens all.

      February 20, 2017

THE WORK BEFORE THE WORK

The work before the work:

Planting

And gratitude

And prayer.

Also the tending,

Also the

Breathing in

And breathing out.

     December 2, 2016

WEATHER

I wonder if

As one grows older,

Weather grows more

Interesting.

I revel in its fierceness,

Its extremes,

Its bold clear beauty.

Harsh then gentle.

Does it ask of me

That I unleash

Those powers

In myself?

Is that the reason

That I glory in its power?

  December 25, 2015

FRUITION

Things are coming
To fruition—
Oddly, in a winter season—
Almost solstice—
One cannot know
The seasons in advance—
Sometimes life's
Bounty comes
Amidst the winter snows—
Sometimes the harvest
Comes in spring.

December 20, 2014

ARMS TOWARD HEAVEN

It seems

The trees—

Especially oaks—

Reach up

Their arms

Toward Heaven—

In gratitude

For light—

Or celebration

Of the day.

It's clearest

What they're doing

In the winter months

When branches

Are all bare—

Their joy—

Like ours

In later seasons

Of our lives—

Is evident in

their stark silhouettes.

February 20, 2016

AS IF

I'd lived here always,
I am settling
Into the nature
Of this place—
As if I'd come
From here
Only to come back here,
I recognize
This place as home—
As if this circle
Of fond faces,
An extended family of sorts,

Always gathers every morning

After breakfast

To commune,

Commiserate

And swap our

Hopes and joys

And wonderings—

As if the world

Could always

Be like this,

Because today

It is.

December 7, 2016

SPRING

No One Swims Alone

THE CHANGE OF SEASONS

The change of seasons,
Marked by birds—
The Tundra swans
Have left, gone north—
The geese, so noisy on
The creek in wintertime,
Are nowhere to be seen—
But osprey hover overhead
Watching for fish and crying,
And blue heron wades with
Silent patience.

Some people think the flowers

Herald Spring—

For me,

It is the birds.

     March 24, 2017

I SIT WITH THE CREEK

I sit with the creek
And it allows me
To sit with myself—
Low energy,
Low water,
All the same.
A natural shift in flow,
Driven by winds
And storms,
Marked by the tides.
I can't complain
Of what I see

Out on the creek—

It's natural.

So with myself—

The pouring forth

Of these last days,

Of facing into storms,

Now shifts to days

Of a low tide.

How long?

No way to tell.

I sit with empty creek.

I sit with empty self.

     March 4, 2017

STEADY IN THE RAIN

Something happened
Monday morning—
A shift in weather:
What had been
A season of appreciation,
In just a moment
Shifted to a season of dismay.
I'll never know what touched it off,
Because he will not say.
Perhaps he has no clue.
Like any other storm,
We ride it out

Until skies clear.

Since it's not useful

To him that we talk,

There's no way

I can know

When I should

Seek a shelter

From oncoming storms.

I learn to stand

With patience

And unmoving,

Steady in the rain.

   March 24, 2016

ANGELS

We travel—
Angels
On each others
Shoulders—
Lifted, buoyed,
Encouraged and
Pressed forward,
By the words we've shared,
Worlds we've explored,
Struggles laid bare—
We enter
Heavy laden—

We leave

Bedeviled as before,

Or even more bedeviled,

But with angels

As our company.

      March 15, 2015

NO ONE SWIMS ALONE

No one

Swims

Alone:

An old rule

In the home

Where I

Grew up

Along the lake.

Safety first.

No one

Swims alone,

No matter
What their
Strength.

So here,
As well,
In azure seas,
For those of us
Swimming
Through losses
In our lives,
No one
Should
Swim
Alone.

      March 24, 2004

MIRACLES

A daughter,
Present, vibrant,
Beautiful,
As if like the geese
And swans
That drop out
Of the sky,
And light upon
Our pond,
A joy of nature—
Unexpected,
Celebrated,

Loved for the season,

Sometimes brief,

That brings

Them here.

    March 8, 2016

POSSIBILITIES AND LIMITS

The possibilities

Lie out there—

As if on a horizon—

Close or distant—

But the limits,

Those too

Lie ahead

To be explored,

And lived—

Not so much

Limiting

As might have seemed

At first,

But real,

And tangible,

And human—

Like a puzzle

That life

Offers us

To work with

And complete—

A picture

That emerges

Over time,

Made of the

Possibilities,

That fit

Within the limits.

March 23, 2015

WHEN DO WE EAT GRANDMA?

The comma
Matters—
Every little
Point has
Meaning—
Even the
One you
Are reluctant
To speak—
That too.

March 13, 2016

SPACE IS EVERYTHING

Space is everything—
Silence is all—
Solitude brings life—
The things that we
Would label nothing—
Turn out to be
Everything
Instead.

      April 2, 2017

BEST NOT

Best not

To take our eyes

Off of the world—

We will miss

Seeing things

As they now are—

The sun on osprey—

It has white feathers

Underneath its eyes—

The mirrored creek's

Repeat of trees and clouds—

The visual silence, peace—

Best not to take our

Eyes off of our world,

In fascination with

The headlines

And fears everywhere,

Reports of yesterday and fears

We must anticipate tomorrow—

The osprey floating in the sun

Across the way

Turns out to have

No shred of

Fear, of "henny penny."

We on the other hand

Become consumed

By echoes of that childhood verse—

"Henny Penny the sky is falling"

We keep repeating it,

Our distracted eyes
Averted from the osprey

Flying high against the sky,
White feathers underneath its eyes.

April 4, 2017

LONG AFTER

Long after

The time

A tree

Seems most

In its prime,

It is in

Unforeseen ways

Shaping things

In partnership

With earth,

And nature's processes,

Still part

Of an unfolding

Possibility.

    April 21, 2016

SOME DAYS

The fears recede—
No reason
In particular—
Nothing has changed—
The CT scan
Report's not back—
My heels still ache—
There's work
That's looming,
Still undone—
But fears are gone—

As if some angel

Has caught

Every small anxiety

In a fine net—

And flown away

With them.

How is it

Such a change occurs?

The weather?

Or the morning?

Or the rest?

Or is it

Quiet work

Of angels?

April 18, 2015

A SMOOTHER ROAD

The CAT scan
Came back clear
Of everything
We might have feared—
And so the travels,
And the work,
That lies ahead
Mean traveling
A smoother road
Than might have been.
I was exhausted yesterday
By the relief.

And now I'm startled

By the restful sense

Of what at other times

Might have appeared

As heavy work—

Which in the shadow

Of these weeks behind us,

Appears simply

As an opportunity

To live this joy.

      April 19, 2015

GIFTED

Life has gifted me—
More unexpectedly this season—
Who would have thought
It likely, possible?
Life turned a corner,
Opened up a door
That had seemed closed.
Gave me these times
In England
As a native—
With a native—
Tracing back roads with

Surprising ease,

Not troubled by the

Unfamiliar, the

Roundabouts running

The wrong direction—

Not troubled

By anything at all.

    May 18, 2016

A NEW LIGHT

The new light
Of a new day—
Sun breaking through,
Splashing against
The tree trunks,
Roof tops, and a
Long white fence
Far, far away;
Irrepressible light,
Unstoppable,
Like life,

Taking us
With it,
Drawing us along.
April 10, 2014

CLEAR VIEW

I have a clear view

Up the creek,

Toward the south;

The water glassy,

Pewter, green,

The trees repeated in

The mirrored stream;

Yet branches broken

By slight ripples

On the surface

Of the water—

Nature at play

With her own beauty,

Breaking patterns

With the wake of three

Slow silent geese,

Floating about;

The colors changing

With the light

Of every moment,

Nothing returning,

Nor need return

Exactly as it was;

Always the

Signature of life

As nature writes it,

Is the change

And the unwavering,

Together.

      April 19, 2014

DANCING IN THE WINGS

We're not

Beginning

Anything—

We're simply

Joining processes

Of life

That flow

Through time—

We ride the

Flow of tide,

The crest of wave—

We are creating

By participating

In the energies

That flow through us,

Call out to us.

We are simply

Joining forces

Dancing in the

Wings of what

We think

Is center stage.

April 19, 2014

I CANNOT TELL

I move between

Seeing the poetry

As self-indulgence,

And spotting something else

That it might be—

I cannot tell.

I just keep writing.

I didn't know my mother,

So perhaps I've come to write,

To know myself,

And in the writing

Thus to know the bits of her

Lodged in the me

Who writes

The poetry.

Perhaps the

Mother who was

So hard to know,

So secretive,

Is hiding still—

In me—

And peeks out

Through the poetry.

      April 21, 2014

TRAIN

A distant
Train
Whistles,
The wheels
On rails
Sound like
A slow
Ocean roar,
Muffled
But evident.
Someone
Is on a

Journey home.

Someone is

Lost.

Someone

Is waiting

At a station.

The whistle sounds

Its warning

At the crossing.

The whistle

Sounds.

     May 29, 2005

EMPTY DAYS

Empty days.

Silence.

Wondering.

No projects.

Just moving

As the spirit

Moves—taking

What comes

To hands—

No restlessness,

No great intent—

Just being,

Peaceful,

Saying yes

To life

As it unfolds.

May 30, 2015

CLEAR SKY

Clear sky,
Soft breeze,
Low tide,
Bird sounds,
Sunlight.
An osprey cries,
Then silence—
These words
Upon the page,

so simple,

The world

Miraculous.

    May 19, 2017

WILD SPACES

No one of us

Could have created

What all of us

Have built

Together.

That connection

Is timeless,

Like tides

And seasons.

Life unfolding

In the wild,

Wild spaces

Of our lives.

May 30, 2016

A SECRET

I am not

Ready yet

To leave

This life—

And yet

I know

The day will come—

When like

The heavy heron

Taking flight

I will go

Willingly

And seemingly

Without an effort.

That knowing

Makes each

Moment a

Fine treasure—

As if I harbor

Some deep truth,

A secret,

That makes all else

Shine with light.

March 10, 2015

A RISING TIDE

A rising tide
Is filling the creek
And a line of geese
Having endured
The season of
Grey frozen water,
Now float past
In silence
On the still
Pewter surface,
As the dawn
Leaves its brief

Pastel touches

On a cloudless sky.

The season

That seemed

Unending

Is passing—

As we hoped

It would.

      March 13, 2015

TICKLED

The leaves
Of one small tree,
Tickled,
By the wind,
Look like
They're laughing,
Standing by
Creek's edge,
Waiting for the
Morning sun.
Perhaps they are.

May 5, 2014

SUMMER

So it has always been,

but now we know

A NEW DAY

The hanging plants
Dance, careen,
In the north wind
Off the lake—
Swing, swirl, twist,
They celebrate the
Start of a new day.
As it turns out
A calm still day
Is not the only
Day to celebrate.

July 30, 2016

BIRTHDAY

You write your

Birthdate all

Your life,

On documents

Of one kind

Or another.

And so when

It's your birthday,

You write the date

As if by habit

As you always have—

Not with this year,

But with the one

When you were born.

As if your life is just

Beginning. Which,

Of course, it is.

June 4, 2015

LIGHT

I used to notice
The specific things—
A tree, a barn, a house—
These days it is the light
I see, the way it shifts,
Transforms, bathes,
And creates—the way
It gives new life
To lifeless surfaces—

It is a miracle—
The light,

The transformation,
And my seeing it.

June 6, 2017

UMBRAGE

He says

That I am

Generous—

I don't

Take umbrage

At something that

She does—

An action that

He sees

As thoughtless.

There's so

Much to be

Carried

In this world,

For which

We have no choice,

That picking up

A peck of umbrage

That is optional

Is not something

I choose to do.

　　　June 13, 2015,

OH, THE DAYS OF RAKES AND BROOMS

Oh, the days

Of rakes and brooms—

Before the great inventions—

Leaf blowers and power mowers,

Weed eaters—

Took over neighborhoods.

Lost is the "swish"

Of simple yard work—

The broom rake

And the broom—

Powered by human energy.

No one sweeps

The porch now—

It's the work of

Leaf blowers.

What we have

Swept away

Is silence and

The softer sounds

Of human effort—

Someone working

At a gentle pace,

The swish of broom

Upon the porch boards,

The rake against

The leaves and grass.

June 2, 2017

SOMETHING WAS DROPPED

Something was dropped

And nothing was said....

He was talking about

The grease spot

On the front porch

Floor boards.

But I was left

With a much

Larger question:

How many times

In life

Might that be true:

Something was dropped

And nothing was said.

> July 8, 2016

FISH FLIES

Fish flies—
Some call them Mayflies—
Dance like diamonds
In the sun,
High above
The lake.

Last night
At dusk
They filled the air, gray,
Millions of them,
Darting down, then up,

In swarms and clouds,
Moving like tiny
Winged kites
Each without a string.

But in the morning's sun
They turn
To diamonds,
Shooting stars,
Their dizzying rise
And then descent,
A mesmerizing
Annual ritual—
A solstice celebration.

They live a day,
Only one day,
Like this.
     June 21, 2017

EXPECTATION

I lay down
Judgement,
Expectation,
Worry—
And feast on
Moments
Full of life.

June 17, 2015

FOREVER

I could
Sit like this
Forever—
Waiting
For a fish
To jump—
Watching
The water's surface
Changing.
Each moment
I am present
To the world

Like this

Is an

Eternity.

I could sit

Like this

Forever.

June 14, 2015,

STORM COMING

Seagulls now
In sunny splendor—
Warm air,
An eastern breeze
Promises a storm
But not yet,
Not here,
Not now.
We know
It's coming
But we soak
Up sunshine

And soft air.

We've learned

Over the years

That it's

The only way

To live.

June 22, 2015

JUST YESTERDAY

Just yesterday

We were that age—

Walking along

The road talking—

Him with a

Paper cup of

Coffee, sipping;

The two of them

Looking at the roses

We have planted

This year,

As I turn 70

And you turn 75.

Yesterday we kayaked

Into town for coffee

And some groceries,

And but for one man

Helping us—

He pushed your kayak,

Fully loaded

With the groceries—

And you—now

Weighing more

Than you did

After surgery

Four months ago—

He launched you out,

Afloat, into the river—

Except for that,

We made the trip

All on our own—

Just yesterday

We were that age.

July 5, 2015

SECOND NATURE

Sometimes

The things

That have been

Second nature

Aren't—

Prompted by

Injury,

A loss,

Some aching change,

Depression—

As if we

Have to learn

Our way, slowly,

Back to our self.

It is a lonely path—

So solitary

It cannot be spoken of,

Until we have arrived

Back home.

June 30, 2014

NEIGHBOR

I wish that I were there
To sit with her,
When he goes
Into surgery,
When he comes out;
In earlier and simpler
Times, good friends
Were always there,
Next door.
Now the joys
That give us freedom—
A cottage in a

Distant state,

A summer home

Up on the Cape,

Disrupt a pattern

Closer to the heart:

The pattern of

Unchanging closeness,

The neighbor

Always

Just across the way.

June 15, 2014

CELEBRATE

(for the Detroit man in the pink suit)

Celebrate the elders

Who stay long among us—

Give up wishing

Them to be

As they once were

Or as we'd want to be—

Were we their age but perfect—

And notice

Who they have become—

With a respect

Approaching

New appreciation—

Fresh eyes

For old souls—

Read as you can,

Their faces,

As old books,

Great classics—

Wondering

What mysteries lie within.

Hold them,

As signed originals,

With gentleness,

Great care.

July 14, 2015

WE KNOW

These are days
Like no other—
Each a gem—
So it has
Always been—
But now we know.

August 2, 2015

NATURE'S DANCER

An oak leaf

Twirls

The distance

To the ground,

Round

And round

And round;

Nature's ballet dancer

Coming finally

To rest
On the dry grass.

Just this one dance;
So with us all.

August 8, 2015

PRUNING

If you

Prune dead branches

From the dogwood,

The hummingbirds

Have no place left

To stand.

It is the leafless,

Deadwood

Offers them

A spot to rest.

A clear spot

For their

Tiny feet—

A place to

Rest their wings.

    August 15, 2014

HOME

Home in the mountains,
Or home by the sea—
Longing for islands
Or farm land or trees—
The soul knows its place:
With the cry of a seagull,
I'm home.

August 6, 2017

I WRITE

I write

To trace

The path of life—

The curious path

Unfolding and

Insisting,

Weaving—

I write so

I will notice

And bear witness

To the voice of

God, or nature,

Or our care

For one another.

Neither fear

Nor pain

Nor loss

Can still

The movement

Of the pen

Toward that light.

August 9, 2017

SOLITUDE

I wilt

Without

The solitude—

Like the

Hanging flower basket

On the porch

Without its morning

Cup of water

And a spritzing,

I am limp

Of mind and heart

Without a spacious,

Generous,

Monk-like

Quiet time.

The blooms

That are my

Better self

Shrivel

In chatter,

Company.

I must remember

As I care for

Flower baskets,

Knowing what

They need to live,

So must I minister

To my own self

With solitude.

July 7, 2016

TRAVEL WITH A CANDLE

Travel with

A candle

And the book

That explains

Wildflowers.

Travel with

Sufficient excess

Time

So when

The wood ducks

Climb upon a log

To preen

You can stand still

And honor them

With presence,

As they have

Honored you.

Travel in peace

And pleasure,

Curiosity

And wonder.

Travel as if

You were

Alive

To life.

August 17, 2005

DREAMS

Don't pin
Your dreams
Of place
On others
Being there—
But on your
Yearning to be
There, yourself—
Your heart song,
The calling of
That land,
That lake,

That sky,

The way

That dawn,

That sunset

Leaves you

Awestruck,

The way

The hill

Protects the house.

We are a

Circling species,

Moving,

Moving,

Seeking.

If you have

Found your

Place,

Return to it

As often as you can,
And if life
Offers you the chance,
Settle there.

July 8, 2014

FAMILY

Family is a

Patchwork

Of memory

And DNA—

"You have your

Father's eyes"

She said, when

We first met again

After a half a century

Had passed.

She has her mother's laugh—

And I'd last heard it

Fifty years ago.

Her mother's gone

Mine, too. What

Do we carry from

The DNA? What

Patchwork quilt

Are we still stitching

From our memories?

> August 13, 2017   (on the 40th
>
> anniversary of my mother's passing)

CONNECTIONS BREAK

Connections break.

In time

They can

Grow back—

If they're allowed to.

One must believe

It's possible,

Or even likely.

Over time.

One must believe

And seek the signs.

August 23, 2017

GIVING UP THE EGG SHELLS

I'm giving up
The egg shells—
The kind you have
To walk on to avoid
Some upset in the other—
Or to make something OK
That really isn't.
I've taken eggs
Out of my diet—

No reason

To keep walking

On the shells.

    August 23, 2014

IT IS A TIME

It is a time

To welcome,

To be kind,

To be unduly generous.

Because the seamy

Meanness of the world

Lies so exposed,

Our work

Is to expose

The kindness.

August 20, 1017

NORTH TOWARD AUTUMN

A flock of geese
Fly high,
Winging north
Toward autumn,
And so are we,
Always,
Enjoying some late
Harvest in our lives,
Winging north
Toward autumn and
The falling leaves,

Preparing

For the winter's dormancy—

Hoping for yet

Another spring.

August 16, 2016

AUTUMN

Have we got the compass

setting right?

WET WEATHER

Lots of new growth

Comes out of

Summers

When it's wet—

People complain and

Carry on about

Miserable weather—

Plants just silently

Put on new growth.

    September 12, 2015,

THINGS FALL

Yesterday things fell—

For no good reason—

Things just

Dove off of the

Edge of other things—

The six foot plant

In heavy pot

Toppled off

A platform in the

Garden of the coffee shop—

I watched it go—

Nothing had touched it.

And then back home,

The light, airy meringues

Fell on a single tiny spice jar

Which then toppled on the

Corner of a plate,

Which then exploded

Into pieces

Sending shards

In all directions.

After that

I was quite careful—

Noticing it seemed

To be

A day

When

Things fell down.

September 12, 2015,

LOGIC

If a policeman

Is allowed

To shoot to kill

When he's afraid

Of someone,

("He feared for his life", they say)

And if a policeman

Has an ingrained and

Unconscious fear

Of dark-skinned men,

Then a policeman can

With full support of law

Shoot a man because he's Black.

How simple is that?

Very simple.

We see it daily.

How do we change it?

Repeated, required,

De-sensitizing experiences

For all police.

And if it takes five or six

Rounds, one round after another,

To stop this violence, that's what it takes.

September 20, 2017

BROWN RIVER

The river is brown,

Rushing, full—

Days of rain,

Like the pelting

Of ugly news,

Day after day,

Police gone free

After shooting

Black men,

Because they are

Afraid of them,

An ugly racist wave,

Bigoted leadership

Masking as strength,

Unleashed like hurricanes

And earthquakes all around us—

A relentless cold rain

Of words and violence,

Like the pelting rains here.

No surprise

That the river

Runs brown,

And full

And raging.

      September 21, 2017

UNSETTLED

Unsettled,

I write poetry.

Lost, I lay down

Words that

Steady me.

How does the

Healing happen?

I don't know.

I only know

I write

Because I must.

November 30, 2016

THE 2016 ELECTION

There are
Many places
To be
After a great
Loss:
Despair,
Commitment,
Depression,
Healing,
Motionless,
Stunned,
Off and away.

It's generosity

To honor

All those

Sanctuaries,

As if each

Is a different

House of prayer—

To let each be,

To not insist

That every true believer

Worships

In the way

I do.

November 22, 2016

GUILTY AT THE PLEASURE

"Self-indulgent"
Was the word
That popped up
Yesterday—
Feeling guilty
At the pleasure
Of the poetry—
Feeling that
Amidst the turmoil
Of the world,
The focus of the poetry
Upon the personal,

The tiny story

Of my heart,

My soul,

My wonderings—

Was insignificant,

Too little social value when

Compared to causes

Others live for—

A tiny canvas—

Like a little painting

Monet might

Have done

For himself alone.

In Paris I remember

The vast wall—

The sweeping canvasses

Of water lilies.

Yet it must be

Monet did sketches—

And tiny works

That spoke to him

As powerfully of how

He saw the world

As did his walls

Of water lilies.

September 15, 2015

OFFER

What do I have
To offer now?
A thousand
Different people
At a hundred different
Points in life,
Responding to
That question,
Would generate a
Cornucopia
Of gifts, of offerings.
Yours? It only

Needs to be

What you

Alone can bring.

What makes your

Heart sing,

Feeds the world.

September 23, 2015,

TOO MUCH

Too much.
We do too much
If we keep doing
What we once have done
Because back then
It was such fun—
It brought such joy.
Great wisdom lies
In laying things
Aside before they
Lose all sweetness,
All real appeal.

It calls for

Wise anticipation

And appreciation.

A discipline

That comes

With time.

September 27, 2015

I AM WHAT I AM

I am what I am—
Without apology
For my kindness—
Nor for my
Blood-hound sense
Of smell,
Nor for my
Losing steam before
The project that I
Launched with
Wild enthusiasm
Is wrapped up.

I am what I am—

Slightly off balance

From a touch of vertigo,

But steady as she goes

In storms

And in the unexpected—

Grateful for the gifts

And graces

That I bring to life.

October 22, 2014

EACH WALK A PRAYER

Each walk
A prayer,
A celebration,
Honoring
The earth
I walk on,
And the miracle
Of muscle, bone,
The body walking.
Each step an alm
Laid on an altar,

In recognition of

The gift it is

To place one foot

Before the other.

     September 11, 2014

THE PRIZE

Maybe
It's the poetry
That is the
Legacy—
Not the
Old brown
Shingled cottage
On the lake,
Or Mother's
Bright fiesta dishes,
Or hand-knit sweaters
With complex designs.

Wouldn't it

Turn out as

A surprise, if it's

Simply the poetry

That takes

The prize?

September 9, 2015,

SAFE PATH IN

A safe path in

Is great—

A way to offer

Challenge—

We happen on

Our courage

If the path is safe,

The door is open,

The way is

Welcoming,

The introductions warm—

In such conditions

We confront
Life's challenges
Wholeheartedly
And honestly,
Together and alone—
Solitary,
In community—
There we find
Within ourselves,
The courage
That we did not know
Was ours.

November 21, 2014

WHIMSY

Yesterday I found a nut,

Lying in gravel,

The kind that fits

Upon a bolt. I picked

It up and tucked

It in my pocket,

Thinking with a smile

That it might come in handy—

Just in case

There is a bolt

Out of the blue.

You never know.

It's always good

To be prepared.

September 3, 2015,

MIND

Not much poetry is on my mind—

Productive mind

Is running everything—

Planning, producing,

Scheduling and getting

Organized. Poet mind

Is waiting for her moment,

Time to shine,

To speak, to step

Into the light.

She's patient,

And these days,

Compassionate, about her

Serious, focused sister,

That other mind—

It's all about the season—

It's just a

Matter of the time.

October 11, 2014

SETTLED

Settled
Here in Dorset
In an old
Sawmill—
And settled
In a larger
Sense—
Within myself—
Within my life.
Earlier in life
We settle down—
When there is

Something owed,

We settle up.

But here and now

It's just plain "settled"

That describes

My heart and soul.

I'm settled.

How it has come to be

I'm not quite

Sure at all—

Acceptance and

Appreciation?

Age? Allowances

For being human,

Perhaps, or

Just the wisdom

Comes with time

On Earth—

Like soil,

Like rock,
Like Earth herself,
I'm settled.

    September 5, 2015,

WALKING TOWARD WAYTOWN

Walking toward

Waytown—

The distant English village,

With its pub—

Is nowhere

Near the same as

Walking to Waytown—

We miss our lives

By trying to arrive

Instead of setting out

In a direction—

When all that really matters

Is the traveling itself,

And have we got

The compass setting right.

September 15, 2016

RESTAURANT IN STRATFORD ON AVON

Frail and elderly—

Out for lunch—

Trying to be

Normal when

Whatever normal was

Has been

Long gone—

He calls her

"Thankless bitch"

Because she won't

Finish her fish and chips,

And she acts as if
Nothing out of the
Ordinary is happening—
Perhaps it's not.
She reaches across
The restaurant table
To hold my hand
And asks if I would like
Her tartar sauce.
Saints save us
From such shabby,
Heartless days—
They come to us,
This couple does—
As harbingers:
Don't wait
Too long

To get

Whatever help

You need.

September 22, 2015,

WHAT IS IT ABOUT TREES?

What is it

About trees and

Clouds and sky—

That as a child

I would lie

For hours

Underneath the

Pine out front,

Eyes open,

Looking up,

And wondering.

That was sixty years ago—

And yesterday,

On holiday

In England,

When clouds

Were mammoth,

Regal, the

Sky a perfect blue,

I tried it once again,

And it was every bit

As beautiful

As years ago,

And far away,

And I was for a moment,

Just as I was then,

At home.

       September 23, 2016

HARMING AND HEALING

Nature puts the
Things that harm
And those that heal
Together; stinging nettles
And the weed that takes
Away the sting grow
Side by side—
And mounds of
Blackberries among

The vicious brambles.
Life's a tangle,

So too the hedgerows
Where blackberries hide.
September 11, 2014

EXPLAINING

It's difficult to
Tell someone
About our gathering—
A space for
Tired people
To renew,
Connect,
Collect ideas,
Practices,
To steady them
For the long road
Ahead.

To form a "conga line",

Processional,

A pilgrimage,

A family—

To move together

And to move

This world ahead.

November 1, 2015

I'M UNEMPLOYED
and I've stopped looking

"I'm unemployed
And I've stopped looking,"
He said, smiling.

In this unusual space,
We know ourselves,
Each other,
Only as presence
In a quiet circle—
We haven't been
Together in the

Decades of the work

That each of us

Experiences as

Who we are—

And so gathered

Together

Thus,

In quiet

And in listening,

We see each other—

Not in role

But in our spirit garb—

Each of us

Struggling

To set aside

The cloak

Of other times,

Of other selves.

     November 23, 2014

ELDER AND YOUNGER

We are saving

Each other's lives—

Elder and younger—

Creating lifelines,

Bridges—

Over time

And over generations—

Learning,

Listening to life,

Embracing.

      November 1, 2015

THE ENGLISH GARDEN

Like so many things in life

That seem familiar,

The English garden

Turns out not to be—

The English Ivy, yes,

The same,

But that odd tree

That always looks

About to die—

Its leaves wrinkled

And shriveled—

Is doing fine.

They call it "cobnut."

And the strange flat

Heavy fern with purple

Seed strips on the

Underside that look

Like they were written by a

Felt-tipped pen,

Are nothing like our own—

And here the dandelions

Are left to flower—

Not seen as weeds—

All that is very strangely

Foreign and exotic.

And the English words,

This old language

That we oft mistake

For our own tongue,

Is not.

And the assumptions,

Always assumptions,

Trip us up,

Like some foreign botanical.

September 3, 2014

THE PRACTICE OF ANXIETY

Instead of wondering,

I'm worrying—

Instead of musing

I'm concerned.

Instead of living

In the glory

Of the moment

I am in,

I'm slipping back,

Then racing forward,

As if some balance wheel

Is asking for repair—

As if I'm in a

Fight with time.

October 25, 2016

MARGINS

What has life

Given me today

But only margins

In which

I can write,

Like Martin Luther King Jr.

The white space

On the edges

Of a document

Designed

For something else,

Is all I can

Command,

All that I have

At hand.

Perhaps

The margins

Are sufficient,

Though,

In moments,

When there's

Clarity of voice,

Perhaps

We only need

The margins,

Perhaps

We only need

Our voice.

     October 2, 2009,

WHAT CAN A POEM DO?

What can
The poem do?
It opens
To a space
Of wondering,
And wandering
With spirit-mind—
And there
The poem
Can do anything.

September 4, 2015,

STILL, STILL WATER

Still, still water—
The autumn creek
A mirror it is:
I kayak on the sky,
Over the cirrus clouds,
I float upon the oaks,
Their burnished orange—
The yellow, gold.
The red of fall,
Is what I paddle over;

The world is

Upside down—

Spectacular.

    October 28, 2014

POSTSCRIPT

THE ROAD CALLS

Little more

To write

Right now,

The road calls,

Details,

Bags to pack.

Another day

I'd tarry here

And let my

Thoughts stray

As they may—

But just today—

Tomorrow too,

The schedule is

The master

To the poet

And the page.

     April 18, 2006

MIRACLES

(if we hold out for angels)

Miracles are everywhere around—

The fire blazing in

The old stone fireplace,

That started up

Without a match

This morning,

Taking light from coals

Of yesterday—

With one page of the

Local paper wadded up

And four pine cones from

The white pine out front—

So little human effort—

So with the miracles

Of every kind—

If we hold out

For angels to be

Harbingers

Of miracles,

We overlook

Their spirit

In the flames.

June 21, 2014

THE DEEP WELL AND
THE ECHOES

The waiter is a New Orleans echo

Of my daughter's Brooklyn love;

My colleague in the field of elder care

Is so like my husband's surgeon

That it throws me sometimes;

I pass a man along the hall

And my Dad, now decades gone

Seems suddenly beside me;

An acquaintance waves hello

And in his eyes I see the glance

Of an early love.

People who are echoes

Of the people we have lost,

Or have lost track of,

Echoes of the people who are distant

From our day to day,

They reappear like apparitions

Of warm comfort and connection

In our lives.

When the well is deep and full

They come to drink with us,

In silence and shared gratitude—

As if in reappearing

In our mind's eye, heart's eye,

They are every bit as present

As they once were—

Like a tune we find we're humming

Unexpectedly and unaccountably—

They are every bit as close and real—

Which certainly they are,

And always are—
In moments when
The well is deep.

November 2, 2017